STORYBOOKS
TEACH WRITING

by Murray Suid

Illustrated by Marilynn G. Barr

This book is for Elnora and Scott Chambers

Publisher: Roberta Suid
Design: David Hale
Copy Editor: Carol Whiteley
Typesetting: Santa Monica Press
Consultants: Sue Krumbein, Wanda Lincoln

Excerpt from ALEXANDER AND THE TERRIBLE, HORRIBLE, NO GOOD, VERY BAD DAY by Judith Viorst. Reprinted with the permission of Atheneum Publishers, an imprint of Macmillan Publishing Company. Text copyright © 1972 Judith Viorst.

Excerpt from CORDUROY by Don Freeman. Copyright © 1968 by Don Freeman. Used by permission of Viking Penguin, a division of Penguin Books USA Inc.

Excerpt from CURIOUS GEORGE by H.A. Rey. Copyright 1941, © renewed 1969 by H.A. Rey. Reprinted by permission of Houghton Mifflin Company. All rights reserved.

Excerpt from THE DAY JIMMY'S BOA ATE THE WASH by Trinka Hakes Noble. Copyright © 1980 by Trinka Hakes Noble. Used by permission of Dial Books for Young Readers, a division of Penguin Books USA Inc.

Excerpt from GOODNIGHT MOON by Margaret Wise Brown, © copyright 1947 by Harper & Row, Publishers, Inc. Reprinted by permission of HarperCollins Publishers

Excerpt from HORTON HATCHES THE EGG by Dr. Seuss. Copyright 1940 by Dr. Seuss. Copyright renewed 1968 by Audrey S. Geisel and Karl Zobell, trustees under the trust agreement dated August 27, 1984. Reprinted by permission of Random House, Inc.

Excerpt from IF YOU GIVE A MOUSE A COOKIE, copyright © 1985 by Laura Joffee Numeroff. Reprinted by permission of HarperCollins Publishers.

Excerpt from WHY MOSQUITOES BUZZ IN PEOPLE'S EARS by Verna Aardema. Copyright © 1975 by Verna Aardema. Used by permission of Dial Books for Young Readers, a division of Penguin Books USA Inc.

Excerpt from WILLIAM'S DOLL by Charlotte Zolotow, copyright © 1972 by Charlotte Zolotow. Reprinted by permission of HarperCollins Publishers.

Entire contents copyright © 1994 by Monday Morning Books, Inc.
Box 1680, Palo Alto, California 94302

For a complete catalog, write to the address above.

Monday Morning is a registered trademark of
Monday Morning Books, Inc.

ISBN 1-878279-69-6
Printed in the United States of America
987654321

❖ CONTENTS ❖

❖ INTRODUCTION ❖

Writing a story isn't one job. It's a collection of tasks, including:

- getting ideas
- figuring out where to begin
- creating memorable characters
- writing ear-catching dialogue

Literary models provide exciting starting points for mastering these skills. *Storybooks Teach Writing* shows how to use examples in a holistic and delightful way.

Working with Models

Each lesson features one or a few storybooks that introduce a concept. For example, *Mr. and Mrs. Pig's Evening Out* illustrates key character roles—hero, villain, victim, and fool.

Storybooks provide excellent examples that are readily accessible to children. These models are well-suited to today's busy classroom where each moment is precious. Classics such as *Corduroy* take only minutes to read and are widely available. The Bibliography lists all the books discussed on the following pages. Of course, your favorites, old and new, can also be used.

Teaching Strategies

This book has four parts: Story Ideas, Plot, Characters, and Writing.

As with most creative activities, when it comes to studying literature there is no one right place to begin. Some teachers like to start with ideas, others with characters. Feel free to create your own sequence, and to focus on the topics that best meet the needs of your students.

Each two-page lesson begins with a short introduction that defines the skill. You might read this material aloud, or paraphrase it to suit the comprehension level of your class. Four interrelated activities follow:

- **Model Reading** offers tips for reading aloud the storybooks. For example, before presenting *Horton Hatches the Egg*, you might draw a story chart on the board to help students identify the elements found in every plot, such as conflict and climax.
- **Language Scouting** invites students—working alone or in small groups—to find their own examples in other books, as well as in movies and on TV.
- **Story Writing** presents quick exercises that encourage students to apply what they learned, for example, by writing new dialogue for famous stories. These practices can lead to full-blown stories.
- **Book Exploring** suggests ways to develop literacy as part of an independent reading program.

Using storybooks is an effective way to develop language arts skills. But it's more than that. The method brings joy to students and teacher. How could it be otherwise, when you fill your room with the likes of Jimmy's Boa, Corduroy, Horton, the Cat in the Hat, the Wild Things, and Peter Rabbit?

PART 1

Story Ideas

If a grain of sand enters an oyster's shell, a pearl may form. A similar creative process occurs in humans. When something catches a person's attention, that spark of consciousness—an idea—may stimulate the person to think up a story. Although the number of story ideas is infinite, most fit into one of four categories:

REAL EVENTS Routines, such as making friends, going to school, eating, working, and handling emotions.

FANTASIES Impossibilities, such as animals or objects that behave like human beings.

SPINOFFS New stories based on earlier stories.

VALUES Beliefs or opinions about good and evil.

Few story ideas are purely one type or another. For example, *The Cat in the Hat Returns* is a sequel (a spinoff) that's also a fantasy.

Nevertheless, knowing about the four types can help young writers discover more to write about. This understanding teaches them that they can get ideas by: 1) noticing what's going on around them; 2) paying attention to their dreams and daydreams; 3) reading, going to the movies, and watching TV; and 4) taking stands about right and wrong behavior.

REAL EVENTS

Fiction often begins with everyday matters, such as doing chores, coping with illness, and building friendships. Reality-based stories fall into two groups:

Realistic Stories mirror the way things really are. An example is "The Boy Who Cried Wolf," which is about the kind of prank one might expect from a bored youth.

Exaggerated Stories begin with ordinary happenings, such as finding a lost cat. But then a storyteller twists the facts into an entertaining tale, such as Wanda Gag's *Millions of Cats*, a book which is meant to be disbelieved. Exaggerating may be done to scare readers or to make them laugh. The steps involved in stretching the truth are dramatized in Dr. Seuss' classic, *And to Think That I Saw It on Mulberry Street.*

The storybook models for this lesson are:

The Day Jimmy's Boa Ate the Wash
The Snowy Day

❖ ACTIVITIES ❖

MODEL READING

Clarify the difference between realistic and exaggerated stories by reading aloud and comparing *The Snowy Day* (very realistic) and *The Day Jimmy's Boa Ate the Wash* (definitely a "stretcher"). Ask students which is more believable, and why.

To reinforce the notion that "ordinary" life is rich in story ideas, read aloud other reality-based stories about a variety of topics. Some examples:

Subject	Model
bad days	*Alexander and the Terrible, Horrible, No Good, Very Bad Day*
cities	*The Little House*
families	*Stevie*
fear	*There's a Nightmare in My Closet*

LANGUAGE SCOUTING

On a visit to the library, have students look for reality-based storybooks that deal with events students might know about firsthand—getting lost, losing a tooth, and so on. Later, in small groups, students can read aloud the books to their classmates. In this way they can share their discoveries while practicing oral reading skills.

STORY WRITING

Brainstorm commonplace events that occur in the classroom (working on math, writing stories) or outside school—getting a haircut, sleeping over, losing something, dealing with a telephone salesperson. Choose one such happening and have the whole class collaborate on turning it into an exaggerated story. For example, what if a person getting a haircut had hair that grew faster than the hair cutter could cut it?

After kids get the hang of creatively "stretching the truth," they might write individual tall tales.

BOOK EXPLORING

Have students relate the books they are reading to reality. If a reader had an experience similar to one in a book—for example, moving to a new city or learning how to dive from a high diving board—he or she might compare personal knowledge to the author's description of the event. Which is more real?

FANTASIES

Many popular stories deal with impossibilities:

- animals that talk—*Alice in Wonderland*
- objects that don't obey the laws of physics—*E.T.* (the flying bicycles)
- fabulous inventions—*The Time Machine*
- amazing changes—"Cinderella" (pumpkin into coach)
- extraordinary abilities: *Superman*

The secret to writing successful fantasy stories is to include a healthy dose of reality. For example, while Cinderella's coach is definitely magical, her relationship with her siblings is presented realistically.

In fact, many authors use fantasy as a way to hook the audience so that they'll pay attention to serious and down-to-earth messages. A famous example is Dickens' *A Christmas Carol*.

The storybook model for this lesson is:

Strega Nona

❖ ACTIVITIES ❖

MODEL READING

Ahead of time, talk about things that are real and things that are make-believe. Ask students to listen for examples of each in *Strega Nona*. During or after the reading, students can identify what was real and what wasn't:

Real Things	Unreal Things
help wanted signs	magic pasta pots
people who snoop	pasta floods
disasters	magic songs

LANGUAGE SCOUTING

Have students look for fantasy in storybooks, movies, and TV shows. TV commercials are also a source, for example, objects that use language (singing toilets), people who fly through the air, and babies who talk like adults.

STORY WRITING

Brainstorm a list of ordinary objects. Then have students turn the objects into things that behave in a fantastic manner:

Object	Fantastic Behavior
bicycle	can balance by itself
car	goes forever without needing gas
clock	can speed up or slow down time
faucet	emits any fluid wanted—juice, milk, etc.
football	can sail wherever it wants, like a bird
pencil	can write stories by itself
snow	can form itself into snow figures
wallet	contains endless amounts of money

Individual students or small groups then pick one fantastic thing and write a story about it. The story might tell how the main character gets the object (finds it, buys it, trades for it) and what happens when the character uses the thing.

BOOK EXPLORING

Each student reads a fantasy book such as *The Phantom Tollbooth*. Students then discuss, orally or in writing, how the fantasy fits into the plot. They must also tell whether or not the author tries to explain how the fantastic elements of the story occur. See page 14 for a list of fantasy books.

When a story is popular, its writer or another writer may create a new story based on the old one. The first story is called the "original." The new story is called a "spinoff." There are several kinds of spinoffs:

An **adaptation** translates the original material into a new format. For example, a nursery rhyme might be told as a short story.

A **sequel** puts the main characters from the original story into a new story, which is the sequel. ("Sequel" comes from a word that means "to follow.") Sometimes the sequel picks up where the earlier story left off. Other sequels tell new adventures starring the old characters. When a book has more than one sequel, the books form a series.

A **parody** turns a serious story into a joke. The trick in writing this kind of story is to make the villain seem silly rather than dangerous.

A **transformation** changes the original in one important way. For example, an old story might be moved to modern times, or the villain in the original story might be presented as the hero in the spinoff. A good example of this is *The True Story of the 3 Little Pigs! by A. Wolf.*

The storybook models for this lesson are:

The Cat in the Hat
The Cat in the Hat Comes Back
George and Martha

❖ ACTIVITIES ❖

MODEL READING

Introduce the lesson by saying something like this: "Often a new story grows out of an earlier story. The earlier story is called the original. The new one is called a spinoff. I'm going to read you two stories: an original and a spinoff. Then we'll compare them to see how they're alike and different."

After reading two stories from *George and Martha* or the two *Cat in the Hat* books, have the class collaborate on making a Venn diagram that shows how the original and the spinoff are alike and different. Elements to consider are: characters, location, theme, and actions.

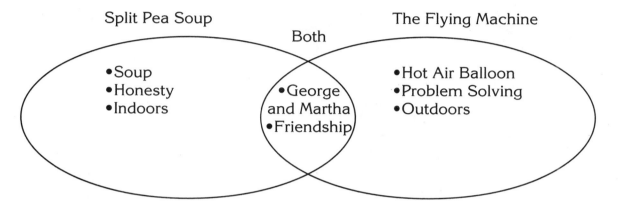

Split Pea Soup

Both

The Flying Machine

- Soup
- Honesty
- Indoors

- George and Martha
- Friendship

- Hot Air Balloon
- Problem Solving
- Outdoors

After completing the diagrams, students might debate the question: Which is better, the original or the spinoff?

LANGUAGE SCOUTING

Have each student look for a sequel on TV (situation comedies, action shows), at the movies, or among a newspaper's comic strips. The language scouts should describe the common elements found in the original and in the sequel.

STORY WRITING

Have students, working alone or in small groups, choose a picture book or a fairy tale and write a sequel to it. The sequel might continue the action in the original, or it might simply be about a new adventure had by the characters from the original.

Another option is for students to write original stories, which they swap with classmates. The partners then write spinoffs based on each other's story.

BOOK EXPLORING

Have students compare and contrast a spinoff with the book on which it was based. These papers or oral presentations might feature Venn diagrams. A list of books with sequels appears on page 14.

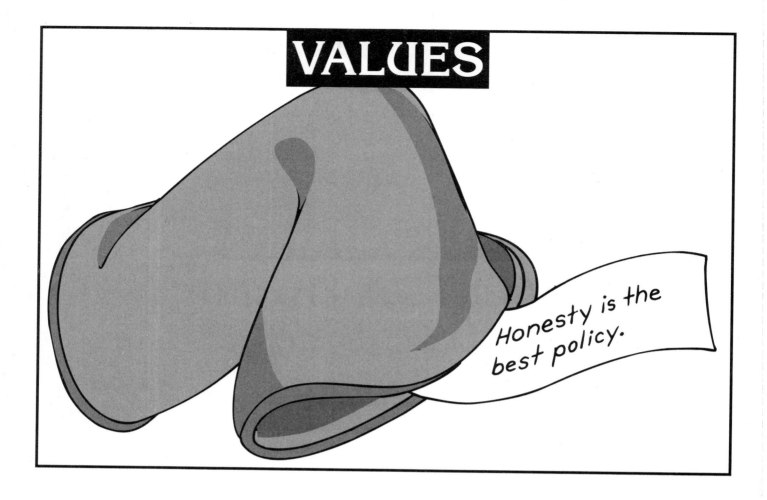

VALUES

Honesty is the best policy.

Almost every story teaches a lesson about how people should behave. Examples of values include:

- A penny saved is a penny earned.
- Haste makes waste.
- Honesty is the best policy.
- Two heads are better than one.
- The journey of a thousand miles begins with a single step.

Some writers don't set out to teach values. The lessons simply grow out of the action.

Other storytellers—for example, those who write fables—begin with the goal of conveying messages about fairness, honesty, hard work, responsibility, or whatever issue they're concerned with. In such stories, the action is meant to dramatize the moral lesson.

Because everyone has opinions about good and evil, values are a rich source of material for generating stories.

The storybook models for this lesson are:

❖

Horton Hatches the Egg
William's Doll

❖ ACTIVITIES ❖

MODEL READING

As a pair, *William's Doll* and *Horton Hatches the Egg* prove that value stories can be serious or silly, realistic or fantastical. After reading each book aloud, have students talk about the values they find. Expect some disagreement. Readers often discover different values in the same story. For example, possible lessons taught by *William's Doll* are:

- Be true to yourself.
- It's OK for a boy to want to develop nurturing skills.
- Persistence pays.

Dr. Seuss states his message more explicitly in *Horton Hatches the Egg*: "An elephant's faithful—one hundred percent." But even in this case, there is room for various interpretations:

- Hard work will be rewarded.
- Don't give up just because people laugh at you.
- Doing the right thing can be difficult.

LANGUAGE SCOUTING

Bring in a variety of storybooks and have students, working alone or in groups, practice spotting values. Some examples:

- *Ira Sleeps Over:* Know yourself.
- *Strega Nona:* Keep your promise.
- *There's a Nightmare in My Closet:* Face your fears head on.

STORY WRITING

Brainstorm a list of values, or use those mentioned above. Have students, alone or with partners, choose a value and write a fable that teaches it. Fables are very short stories that usually feature talking animals. For example:

> A crow in a tree was about to eat a piece of cheese. On the ground below, a fox wanted the cheese. Unable to climb the tree, the fox said, "Crow, I love your musical voice. Will you sing for me?" The crow was so pleased by this praise that it began to sing. But when it did, the cheese fell, right into the fox's mouth. Moral: Don't trust flatterers.

Arnold Lobel's *Fables* (Harper, 1980) is a rich source of models for this assignment.

BOOK EXPLORING

Have students focus on the main value in the books they choose to investigate. In a written or oral presentation, each reader can describe the book's lesson. What actions in the story made the lesson clear? The student might also explain why he or she agrees or disagrees with the value taught by the book.

❖ MORE MODELS ❖

STORYBOOKS

REAL EVENTS
- *The Day Jimmy's Boa Ate the Wash* (field trip)
- *Ira Sleeps Over* (sleep-over)
- *Make Way for Ducklings* (nature)
- *The Snowy Day* (snowstorm)
- *The Tenth Good Thing About Barney* (death of a pet)

FANTASIES
- *Corduroy*
- *The Little Engine That Could*
- *The Little House*
- *Mike Mulligan and His Steam Shovel*

SPINOFFS—SERIES
- *Babar*
- *Curious George*
- *George and Martha*
- *Madeline*

VALUES
- *Alexander and the Terrible, Horrible, No Good, Very Bad Day* (accept the bad with the good)
- *The 500 Hats of Bartholomew Cubbins* (persevere)
- *The Little Engine That Could* (believe in yourself)
- *Mike Mulligan and His Steam Shovel* (look for creative solutions to "unsolvable" problems)
- *Stevie* (appreciate what you have)

FICTION

REAL EVENTS
- *Bridge to Terabithia* (building a friendship)
- *Roll of Thunder, Hear My Cry* (surviving poverty)

FANTASIES
- *Alice's Adventures in Wonderland*
- *The Dark Is Rising*
- *Mrs. Frisbee and the Rats of NIMH*
- *Tuck Everlasting*
- *The Lion, the Witch, and the Wardrobe*
- *The Wizard of Oz*

SPINOFF—ADAPTATION
- *Charlie and the Chocolate Factory* (a play based on the novel)

SPINOFFS—SEQUELS
- *Charlie and the Great Glass Elevator* (based on *Charlie and the Chocolate Factory*)
- *Let the Circle Be Unbroken* (based on *Roll of Thunder, Hear My Cry*)

SPINOFFS—SERIES
- *The Black Stallion*
- *The Borrowers*
- *Chronicles of Narnia* (based on *The Lion, the Witch, and the Wardrobe*)
- *The Dark Is Rising*
- *A Wrinkle in Time*

PART 2

Plot

A story is like a journey. The journey's itinerary is called the story's *plot*. When we tell someone about a story that we've read, heard, or seen, we usually recite its plot. We describe what happens at the main places (settings) that the characters visit along the way. Plot study involves five issues:

MAIN ACTION The most thrilling or important event in the story, for example, Jack's escape down the beanstalk.

STRUCTURE How the parts of the story (such as the trigger event and the climax) fit together to grab and hold the audience's interest.

DURATION The time frame of the story (an hour, a day, a year).

SCENES The individual moments that, taken together, comprise the whole story. Scenes may be labeled according to place (the market scene in "Jack and the Beanstalk") or action (the porridge-eating scene in "Goldilocks and the Three Bears").

SEQUENCE The order used by the storyteller to present the scenes. An event that happened first according to the "clock" may be presented last to the audience. Manipulating the flow of actions is a key skill in the art of creative writing.

MAIN ACTION

Although most stories are filled with a variety of happenings—eating, swimming, and so on—the plot usually centers on one major type of action.

Chases and **Escapes** resemble the game of hide and seek. A character may be trying to escape from the villain ("The Three Little Pigs") or trying to capture the villain.

Contests and **Fights** may focus on brute strength (King Kong versus Godzilla) or celebrate cunning (Red Riding Hood versus the wolf).

Journeys and **Quests** can be one-way trips in which the hero tries to reach a destination ("The Three Billy Goats Gruff"), or they can be round trips that end up back home (*The Wizard of Oz* and *Alice in Wonderland*). Treasure hunts, such as "Jack and the Beanstalk," belong here.

Masquerades feature masks, costumes, and changing identities.

Races work best when the outcome is in doubt. Races can be against the clock ("Rumpelstiltskin").

The storybook models for this lesson are:

Make Way for Ducklings
Mike Mulligan and His Steam Shovel
Ox-Cart Man

❖ ACTIVITIES ❖

MODEL READING

A good way to teach any plot type is to read aloud several models and then help the students discover what the stories have in common. For example, three journey stories—*Make Way for Ducklings*, *Mike Mulligan and his Steam Shovel*, and *Ox-Cart Man*—all involve:

- a destination
- a purpose
- endurance
- a means of transportation (ship, foot)
- interesting sights along the way

Groups of picture books representing several plot types are listed on page 26.

LANGUAGE SCOUTING

Have students look for different types of plots in a variety of storybooks, in TV programs, and in movies. You might make a bulletin board that gives examples of the different kinds of plots.

STORY WRITING

To teach the masquerade, ask students to "Imagine that you could turn yourself into any animal, thing, or person. What would you choose to be?" After hearing their ideas, choose one and brainstorm a list of possible results from making that change. For example, if someone turned into a dog, that person might:

- develop a taste for dog food
- have an adventure chasing a robber
- learn what dogs dream about
- make friends with other dogs

You might write a class story that incorporates some of these possibilities, or students might wish to work individually or in small groups.

A similar approach could be used to teach chases and the other main action types.

BOOK EXPLORING

Have students make oral or written presentations focusing on main actions. For example, after reading a journey story such as *The Wizard of Oz*, a student might make a map showing Dorothy's itinerary: from Kansas to Oz and back to Kansas.

STRUCTURE

Most stories share a common set of plot elements:

The **opening routine** shows characters living their normal lives. For example, Little Red Riding Hood is bringing goodies to her grandmother.

The **trigger event** breaks the routine: Red Riding Hood meets the wolf.

The **conflict** occurs as characters deal with problems caused by the trigger event: Red Riding Hood confronts the wolf in his grandma disguise.

The **climax** is the moment when the story's big question is answered: Red Riding Hood escapes with her life!

The **anticlimax** marks the start of a new routine. The main character is usually different—for example, richer, wiser, or perhaps married.

Hint for teaching young children: Concentrate on just one or two elements at a time. For example, to focus on the "trigger event," ask, "In the story we just read, what happened at the beginning to upset things?" Read another story and ask the same question. List the responses on the board.

The storybook models for this lesson are:

The 500 Hats of Bartholomew Cubbins
Mr. and Mrs. Pig's Evening Out

❖ ACTIVITIES ❖

MODEL READING
Before reading the models, draw the classic story diagram on the board. Define the elements, and illustrate them using a familiar fairy tale.

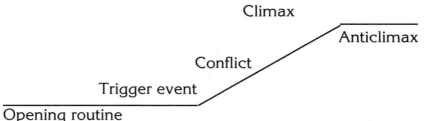

Climax

Anticlimax

Conflict

Trigger event

Opening routine

Read *The 500 Hats of Bartholomew Cubbins* and identify the five elements:

> **Opening routine:** Bartholomew goes to market.
> **Trigger event:** When Bartholomew takes off his hat to honor the king, another hat magically appears.
> **Conflict:** Threatened with beheading, Bartholomew keeps removing hats, but new ones appear.
> **Climax:** The five hundredth—and last—hat is so beautiful that the king buys it from Bartholomew for a bag of gold.
> **Anticlimax:** Bartholomew returns home as a wealthy boy.

When reading *Mr. and Mrs. Pig's Evening Out*, have students identify the elements.

LANGUAGE SCOUTING
Have students identify the five plot elements in a variety of storybooks, or in a film or TV show.

STORY WRITING
Have students brainstorm routines (going to school, doing chores) and then imagine a dramatic change in each one. For example, suppose teachers were not allowed to talk while teaching. Students, working individually or with partners, might write stories that tell what happens after the routine is changed.

BOOK EXPLORING
Have students describe the five plot elements in the books they read. They might use story diagrams (see above) to illustrate their presentations.

DURATION

Writers think carefully about *duration*—how much time passes between a story's beginning and ending. Some stories cover only a few minutes; others span many centuries. Because there is no one right place to start or end a story, two writers inspired by the same incident might create stories with very different durations.

A story's duration is not related to the story's length measured in words or pages. For example, 48-page *Ira Sleeps Over* takes place in half a day, while *The Little House*, a 40-page book, covers many years.

Likewise, the exact same story may be told in a few words or in hundreds of pages. For example, Marianna Mayer's 44-page storybook *Beauty and the Beast* (Four Winds, 1978) covers the same duration as Robin McKinley's 247-page novelized version, *Beauty* (Harper, 1978).

The storybook models for this lesson are:

The Bicycle Man
Ira Sleeps Over
The Island of the Skog
The Little House
Where the Wild Things Are

❖ ACTIVITIES ❖

MODEL READING

Introduce the concept of duration by having the class list events in their lives: sleeping, eating breakfast, going to school, practicing a musical instrument, taking a bath, and so on. Have students rank these events from longest to shortest.

Explain that every story covers a certain amount of time (duration). Tell students to pay attention to the duration of the stories you're about to read. After reading *The Bicycle Man, Ira Sleeps Over, The Island of the Skog,* and *The Little House,* ask: "Which story covered the most time? How can you tell?"

With older students, you might also read and discuss *Where the Wild Things Are.* Part of this story's charm is that it lasts for a few hours in "real time," but about two years of "dream time."

LANGUAGE SCOUTING

Bring in a variety of storybooks or do this activity in the library. Have students, working alone or in small groups, locate three books with very different durations, for example, a day, a week, and a year. (See the list on page 26.) Make a bulletin board that uses the titles to illustrate different story durations.

STORY WRITING

Have students experiment with duration by using the same number of words to describe two events. One event should have a relatively short duration:

- taking a music lesson
- visiting the dentist
- eating dinner

The other event should have a longer duration, for example:

- learning to swim
- going on a family vacation

BOOK EXPLORING

In an informal book discussion circle, students might simply share the time frames of their books: "My book, *Caps for Sale,* covers only an afternoon." A more formal written report about the same book might be titled "An Afternoon in the Life of a Peddler" and could be organized hour by hour.

If your students are reading novels, explain that chapters are really stories within the big story. Students could discuss the duration of each chapter in these novels.

SCENES

Just as a necklace can be strung bead by bead, a writer creates a story scene by scene. The word "scene" refers both to the place where an event happens (the setting) and to what occurs there (the event).

A story can be told in a single scene. For example, the Dutch folk tale of "The Boy with His Finger in the Dike" takes place entirely at the dike. But most stories have several or many scenes. For example, "Little Red Riding Hood" is typically told in five scenes:

1. Inside Little Red Riding Hood's cottage—Little Red gets ready to go.
2. On the path to Grandmother's house—Little Red meets the wolf.
3. In Grandmother's house—Little Red questions the disguised wolf.
4. Outside Grandmother's house—the woodcutter hears a call for help.
5. In Grandmother's house—the woodcutter dispatches the wolf.

To present a story clearly, a storyteller must know how to break the "big story" into smaller scenes. Each scene should itself tell a dramatic story.

The storybook models for this lesson are:

Curious George
There's a Nightmare in My Closet

❖ ACTIVITIES ❖

MODEL READING

Because every story occurs in one or more places, you can teach the concept of scene with any book. However, it's interesting to compare a one-scene story (*There's a Nightmare in My Closet*) with a multi-scene story (*Curious George*).

Before reading the stories, define "scene" as a place where an action happens. List the scenes in a familiar story, such as "Goldilocks and the Three Bears."

To make the notion of scene more concrete, have students list the scenes in a typical day at school. The list should name the place and give the action:

- classroom—studying
- playground—playing
- classroom—more studying
- lunchroom—eating

Ask students to count the scenes as you read the two models aloud. Later, you might point out transitional phrases that help readers follow the action from scene to scene. For example, in *Curious George*, one scene takes place in the cabin of a big ship. The man with the big yellow hat tells George (a monkey):

"Now run along and play, but don't get into trouble."
George promised to be good. But it is easy for little monkeys to forget.
On the deck, he found some sea gulls.

The phrase *On the deck* sets the stage for the next action.

LANGUAGE SCOUTING

Bring in a variety of storybooks and have students look for one book with just a few scenes and another book with many scenes. Older students might graph the number of scenes in several dozen storybooks.

STORY WRITING

Have students write a five-scene description of a typical day in their lives. Because their days might involve more than five scenes, they'll have to decide which are the most important ones.

You can also raise scene awareness by having students write their own single-scene stories, imitating the structure—not the content—of *There's a Nightmare in My Closet*. Topics for one-scene stories include taking a bath, doing a magic trick, eating spaghetti, getting dressed, and watching TV.

BOOK EXPLORING

In book discussion groups, have students compare the way scenes are used in their books. Issues to consider are: the number of scenes in the book; the location of scenes (indoor versus outdoor); the time of scenes (day versus night); and the relative importance of scenes. (Are there scenes that could or should be cut?)

SEQUENCE

Most stories are made up of mini-stories (scenes). "The Three Billy Goats Gruff" consists of three scenes: 1) Baby Billy Goat's encounter with the troll, 2) Mother Billy Goat's encounter with the troll, and 3) Father Billy Goat's encounter with the troll. *Sequence* refers to the order a storyteller uses to present the mini-stories to the audience. There are two frequently used sequences:

Chronological order is the most common sequence. It mirrors the way events unfold in everyday life—first things first, second things second, and so on. For example, in "Jack and the Beanstalk," the sequence begins:

> Jack's mother tells him to sell the cow.
> Jack goes off to sell the cow.
> Jack sells the cow and gets the magic beans.

The sequence obeys the law of cause and effect. One thing leads to the next.

Flashback sequence starts with one event, and then describes an event that took place earlier. A flashback may happen when a character is remembering something. It may also take place during a dream, for example, Scrooge's nightmare in Dickens' *A Christmas Carol*.

The storybook models for this lesson are:

The Day Jimmy's Boa Ate the Wash
Stevie

24

❖ ACTIVITIES ❖

 ## MODEL READING

Introduce "sequence" by presenting the key incidents of a familiar story—for example, "The Three Little Pigs"—in random order:

> The wolf blows down the house of sticks.
> The wolf slides down the third pig's chimney.
> The three pigs leave home to begin their own lives.
> Etc.

Invite students to help you put the events into chronological—by the clock—order. Then tell students you're going to read them a story that presents events in a different type of order: flashback.

After reading *The Day Jimmy's Boa Ate the Wash*, list on the chalk board the major events which it presents:

> Narrator comes home from school and tells Mom the class trip was boring.
> A cow started crying.
> A haystack fell on the cow.
> Etc.

Have students, working alone or in pairs, put the events into chronological order. Then discuss the pros and cons of presenting the story in flashback sequence.

Read *Stevie* to illustrate the use of a short flashback. The flashback occurs near the end, when the hero recalls the good times he and Stevie shared.

 ## LANGUAGE SCOUTING

Have students look for flashback in movies, on TV, and in chapter books. Students might orally share their discoveries: "In last night's episode of 'The Simpsons,' did you see the flashback when Bart remembered his week at camp?"

 ## STORY WRITING

Have students use a flashbacks to describe a real event in their lives. The trick is to begin at the end—"I was covered in mud"—and then introduce the flashback. For example, a true story about a house fire might begin:

> We stood outside our home watching smoke pour out the windows. A friend ran up and asked what was going on. I didn't feel like talking, but her question forced me to remember what had led to this disaster. It all started a week earlier. . .

Older students might experiment by rewriting fairy tales using flashbacks.

 ## BOOK EXPLORING

Have each student, orally or in writing, describe the sequence of a book read independently. The presentation might be illustrated by a series of sketches showing the key scenes in the order they occur.

❖ MORE MODELS ❖

STORYBOOKS

CONTESTS & FIGHTS
- *Casey at the Bat*
- *Mr. and Mrs. Pig's Evening Out*
- *There's a Nightmare in My Closet*

ESCAPES
- *The Amazing Bone*
- *The Red Balloon*
- *The Tale of Peter Rabbit*

JOURNEYS & QUESTS
- *Curious George*
- *Is Your Mama a Llama?*
- *The Little House*
- *Make Way for Ducklings*

RACES
- *Mike Mulligan and His Steam Shovel*

DURATION—AN HOUR OR LESS
- *Casey at the Bat*
- *Goodnight Moon*

DURATION—A DAY OR LESS
- *The Bicycle Man*
- *The Day Jimmy's Boa Ate the Wash*
- *Mr. and Mrs. Pig's Evening Out*

DURATION—A WEEK OR MORE
- *Curious George*
- *Horton Hatches the Egg*
- *Madeline*
- *Make Way for Ducklings*
- *Ox-Cart Man*
- *Stevie*
- *William's Doll*

FICTION

CONTESTS & FIGHTS
- *The Dark Is Rising*
- *The Iliad*

ESCAPES
- *Charlotte's Web*
- *One Hundred and One Dalmatians*

JOURNEYS & QUESTS
- *Alice's Adventures in Wonderland*
- *Around the World in Eighty Days*
- *Charlie and the Chocolate Factory*
- *The Odyssey*
- *Paddle-to-the-Sea*
- *The Wonderful Wizard of Oz*

MASQUERADES & MYSTERIES
- *Mrs. Frisbee and the Rats of NIMH*
- *The Phantom Tollbooth*
- *A Wrinkle in Time*

DURATION—A MONTH OR LESS
- *Alice's Adventures in Wonderland*
- *Charlie and the Chocolate Factory*
- *Julie of the Wolves*
- *The Phantom Tollbooth*

DURATION—A FEW MONTHS
- *Charlotte's Web*
- *Mrs. Frisbee and the Rats of NIMH*

DURATION—ABOUT A YEAR
- *Tales of a Fourth Grade Nothing*
- *Tuck Everlasting*

PART 3

Characters

Exciting actions draw us into stories—arguments, chases, escapes, fights. But when we finish reading, we mostly remember the characters: Cinderella, Lassie, Pinocchio, Amelia Bedelia, Paddington Bear, Mary Poppins, Hansel and Gretel, Charlotte, Rumpelstiltskin, Beauty and the Beast.

When creating a character, a storyteller considers three issues:

ROLE Will the character be a hero, a villain, a victim, or a fool? In some stories, a single character may get a chance to play all four roles.

TYPE Will the character be realistic—the kind of person or animal you might actually meet in everyday life? Or will the character be fanciful—the kind of creature met only in dreams, fantasies, or the distant future?

DEVELOPMENT What actions and speeches will make the character interesting and believable?

In a sense, a storyteller is like a puppeteer. But instead of wood or cloth, the storyteller uses words to create characters and to bring them to life.

ROLES

The characters in a story usually fit into the following categories:

Heroes are the good guys. Readers root for the heroes to succeed: to win the race, escape from danger, find the treasure. The word "protagonist" is sometimes used instead of hero.

Villains are troublemakers. They try to block or harm the hero. Readers hope that these characters will fail to get what they want. The word "antagonist" is a synonym for villain.

Victims are characters who are in danger or who get hurt. Often the hero will try to save a victim, or punish the villain for turning another character into a victim.

Fools are silly or careless characters who unintentionally cause problems for themselves or others. Fools are sometimes the main character in stories that are meant to be funny.

Stories don't always contain all four roles. Most fairy tales feature heroes, villains, and victims. Picture books often omit villains, preferring to focus on the hero's inner struggle with a problem such as loneliness.

The storybook models for this lesson are:

Mr. and Mrs. Pig's Evening Out
The True Story of the 3 Little Pigs! by A. Wolf

❖ ACTIVITIES ❖

 ## MODEL READING
Before presenting the books, list the four roles on the board and explain them to the class. Ask students to suggest examples from fairy tales, songs, movies, and other works. For example: The wolf in "Little Red Riding Hood" is a villain; the grandmother is a victim; the woodcutter is a hero as is Little Red Riding Hood, who deftly unmasks the wolf with her clever questions.

Point out that most people have experienced what it's like to be a hero, a villain, a victim, and a fool. When we encounter each role in a story, we see a different side of ourselves, and maybe get to know ourselves better.

Invite students to look for the four roles in *Mr. and Mrs. Pig's Evening Out*:

- hero: Sorel and, to a lesser degree, the other piglets
- villain: Mrs. Wolf
- victim: Garth (who nearly gets baked)
- fools: Mr. and Mrs. Pig, who fail to notice the rather obvious fact that they've hired a wolf to watch their children

Note that many characters play more than one role. Mr. Pig, for example, acts heroically at the end when he disposes of the wolf.

 ## LANGUAGE SCOUTING
Bring in a variety of storybooks and have students, working individually or in small groups, locate examples of each role. They can share their discoveries orally or in writing. Later, the class might make a bulletin board of real heroes described in newspaper articles.

 ## STORY WRITING
Have students write true stories about times when they played one of the four roles. For example, a child who enticed the family cat down from a tree might write a piece entitled "How I Became a Hero to My Cat." An alternative is for children to write about heroes (or villains) that they have known.

Older students might rewrite a fairy tale or another familiar story in which they turn the villain into the hero or the hero into the villain. As a model, see *The True Story of the 3 Little Pigs! by A. Wolf.*

 ## BOOK EXPLORING
Have students comment, orally or in writing, on the roles played by the main characters in books they are reading. To help them get started, ask questions such as: Who is the hero and what heroic acts does he or she perform? Who is the villain? What did he or she do that is bad?

TYPES

The word "character" may suggest human-like figures, such as Goldilocks and Prince Charming. But there are at least four other types of characters:

Fanciful people include elves, ghosts, monsters, and superheroes. These characters differ from ordinary people in various ways, such as being able to fly (Peter Pan).

Real animals are true to nature. If birds, they fly; if fish, they swim. They don't talk, wear clothes, or do other human activities, such as going to school.

Human-like animals sing, use tools, work, wear clothes, and exhibit human qualities, such as thrift or greed. Some of literature's best-known characters are human-like ("anthropomorphic") animals, including the Cat in the Hat and Peter Rabbit.

Human-like things talk (the Amazing Bone); think (the Little Engine That Could); or have feelings (the Little House). Personification is the art of turning an object (a snowman) into a character (Frosty the Snowman).

The storybook models for this lesson are:

The Red Balloon
Strega Nona
The Tale of Peter Rabbit
The Tenth Good Thing About Barney
There's a Nightmare in My Closet

❖ ACTIVITIES ❖

MODEL READING
Define "character" as "someone or something that plays a part in a story." On the board list the five character types and have students find examples in fairy tales, nursery rhymes, movies, and advertisements.

Real people:	Goldilocks, Jack and Jill
Fanciful people:	the giant in "Jack and the Beanstalk"
Real animals:	Lassie
Human-like animals:	Smokey the Bear
Human-like things:	the talking mirror in "Snow White"

As you read the models, ask students to identify the types of the characters.

The Red Balloon	
Little Boy and the gang of boys	real people
Red Balloon	human-like thing
Strega Nona	
Strega Nona	fanciful person
townspeople	real people
The Tale of Peter Rabbit	
Peter Rabbit	human-like animal
Mr. McGregor	real person
The Tenth Good Thing About Barney	
Barney (the cat)	real animal
narrator, mother, father, friend	real people
There's a Nightmare in My Closet	
narrator	real person
nightmare	fanciful person

LANGUAGE SCOUTING
Bring in a variety of storybooks, and have students look for and share examples of each character type. Older students can extend the hunt into comics, movies, and TV commercials. Post examples on a bulletin board.

STORY WRITING
Have students choose a storybook, and write a new story featuring the same type of character. For example, *The Little Engine That Could*—whose hero is a human-like thing—could inspire a child to write "The Big Airplane That Did."

BOOK EXPLORING
Have students go to the library and find books that include at least one character who doesn't fit in the real-people category. See page 34 for sample titles. Students can later describe the non-human characters orally or in writing.

DEVELOPMENT

Writers use several techniques to create characters.

Labeling or naming: The author simply tells us what kind of character we're dealing with. In the "Three Little Pigs," the villain is called the Big <u>Bad</u> Wolf. In *Where the Wild Things Are*, Max is labeled "Wild Thing!"

Physical detail: The author gives facts about the character's body, clothing, jewelry, manner of walking, and so on. The truly inventive writer often relates a physical detail to the plot. For example, the Big Bad Wolf's big teeth are the final clue that Red Riding Hood needs to unmask the villain.

Action: Behavior often tells much more than appearance. For example, when Jack sells the cow for magic beans, that proves he's a foolish kid. The author doesn't have to label him "foolish." Action is often used to show a character's main trait, such as honesty, nastiness, faithfulness, or cunning.

Dialogue or thought: Talking and thinking can reveal important information about characters. For example, when the giant says, "Fe, fi, fo, fum, I smell the blood of an Englishman. And be he alive or be he dead, I'll grind his bones to make my bread," we know that Jack will be facing someone who isn't a very kind host.

The storybook model for this lesson is:

Horton Hatches the Egg

❖ ACTIVITIES ❖

MODEL READING

Before reading *Horton Hatches the Egg*, list the character-development techniques on the board, and explain them. You might then have students use several or all of the methods to describe themselves, on paper or to a partner:

Labeling:	I'm hard-working.
Physical detail:	I'm short, have curly hair, and smile a lot.
Action:	Watch me dive off the high board.

Ask students to listen for passages that characterize Horton (as kind, loving, etc.) and Mayzie (as selfish, fun-loving, etc). Some examples are:

Labeling:	Sighed Mayzie, a <u>lazy bird</u> . . .
Physical detail:	Poor Horton looked up with his face white as chalk!
Dialogue:	"It's work! How I hate it! I'd much rather play!"
Action:	Then carefully, Tenderly, Gently, he crept Up the trunk to the nest Where the little egg slept.

LANGUAGE SCOUTING

Have students find and share examples of character development in other storybooks. Note: Picture book illustrations may supplement or replace verbal descriptions. Instead of saying a character is weary, the artist may draw the character in a weary pose.

STORY WRITING

Choose one of the character-developing techniques and have all the students give a character a specific trait using that technique. The trait should not be mentioned. For example, if the character is supposed to be smart, the writer might show him or her solving a tough problem. Have students read their descriptions to the class, and see if the listeners can identify the trait.

BOOK EXPLORING

Have students discuss or write about the personalities of the main characters in their books (honest, brave, confused, whatever).

❖ MORE MODELS ❖

STORYBOOKS

REAL PEOPLE
- *Alexander and the Terrible, Horrible, No Good, Very Bad Day*
- *The Bicycle Man*
- *Ira Sleeps Over*
- *Madeline*
- *Mike Mulligan and His Steam Shovel*
- *Ox-Cart Man*
- *The Snowy Day*
- *William's Doll*

FANCIFUL PEOPLE
- *Strega Nona*
- *Where the Wild Things Are*

REAL ANIMALS
- *Caps for Sale*
- *Ox-Cart Man*

HUMAN-LIKE ANIMALS
- *The Amazing Bone*
- *Cat in the Hat*
- *Goodnight Moon*
- *Is Your Mama a Llama?*
- *The Island of the Skog*
- *Mr. and Mrs. Pig's Evening Out*
- *Never Talk to Strangers*
- *The True Story of the 3 Little Pigs! by A. Wolf*
- *Why Mosquitoes Buzz in People's Ears*

HUMAN-LIKE THINGS
- *Corduroy*
- *The Little Engine That Could*
- *The Little House*

FICTION

REAL PEOPLE
- *Bridge to Terabithia*
- *Roll of Thunder, Hear My Cry*
- *Sarah, Plain and Tall*
- *Tales of a Fourth Grade Nothing*

FANCIFUL PEOPLE
- *The Borrowers*
- *The Dark Is Rising*
- *Ghosts I Have Been*
- *The Odyssey*
- *Tuck Everlasting*
- *The Wonderful Wizard of Oz*

REAL ANIMALS
- *The Black Stallion*
- *Julie of the Wolves*

HUMAN-LIKE ANIMALS
- *Alice's Adventures in Wonderland*
- *Charlotte's Web*
- *James and the Giant Peach*
- *The Lion, the Witch, and the Wardrobe*
- *Mrs. Frisbee and the Rats of NIMH*
- *One Hundred and One Dalmatians*
- *The Phantom Tollbooth*

HUMAN-LIKE THINGS
- *The Adventures of Pinocchio*
- *Alice's Adventures in Wonderland*

PART 4

Writing

After a writer gets a good idea and develops it into a plot and dreams up characters to play the parts, the real fun begins: expressing the story in words. This effort involves four issues:

POINT OF VIEW Deciding whether to use the first person (I, we); the second person (you); or the third person (he, she, it, they).

THE LEAD Capturing the reader with a fresh opening sentence or paragraph, preferably something more original than "Once upon a time. . . ."

DESCRIPTION Creating word pictures of the settings and actions.

DIALOGUE Putting interesting words into characters' mouths.

These issues come into play whether the story is written in prose (the language of everyday life) or in rhyme. While modern stories are almost always told in prose, many memorable stories have been cast in rhyme. These range from "A Visit from St. Nicholas" to *Madeline*.

POINT OF VIEW

Every story has a narrator, the person telling the story. The phrase "point of view" refers to the relationship between the narrator, the characters in the story, and the reader. There are three points of view to choose from:

With the **first person point of view**, the narrator uses the pronoun *I* or *we*. This puts the narrator into the action. For example: As I was going to St. Ives, I met a man with seven wives.

With the **second person point of view**, the narrator uses the pronoun *you*. This makes the reader feel like a character in the story:

If you give a mouse a cookie, he's going to ask for a glass of milk.

With the **third person point of view**, the narrator talks about the characters, using their names and the pronouns *he, she, it,* or *they*. This puts both the narrator and the reader outside the action. It's as if they are watching a play or a movie together. Third person is the most common point of view.

The storybook models for this lesson are:

Alexander and the Terrible, Horrible, No Good, Very Bad Day
The Amazing Bone
If You Give a Mouse a Cookie

❖ ACTIVITIES ❖

MODEL READING

Use dramatic readings to introduce "point of view." For example, as you read the first line of *Alexander and the Terrible, Horrible, No Good, Very Bad Day*:

"I went to sleep with gum in my mouth and now there's gum in my hair."

Pretend to pull gum from your hair. Point out that "I" stories don't have to be autobiographical. The narrator, Alexander, is a boy, but the book was written by Judith Viorst, a woman. Once students see that "I" stories can be inventions, many creative possibilities open up. For example, students can research and write first-person stories about their parents' experiences when they were children.

Use *If You Give a Mouse a Cookie* to teach second person. Each time you read the pronoun *you*, point directly to the children. Later, ask students how the "you" makes them feel. Do they like being involved in the action?

Illustrate third person with *The Amazing Bone* or any other third-person book, of which there are thousands. Point out the use of the characters' names and the third-person pronouns.

LANGUAGE SCOUTING

Have students look for and share examples of different points of view in other storybooks (see page 44). Older students might make a collaborative bulletin board of examples found in newspaper or magazine articles and advertisements.

STORY WRITING

To clarify the creative use of first person, have each student choose a narrator other than himself or herself. It might be a friend, a relative, an object, or a make-believe person. Students then use these narrators to describe real or invented experiences. For example, "I am the bathtub in Sandy's apartment . . ."

Older children can explore point of view by rewriting part or all of a third-person story using the first person. For example: "My name is Goldilocks. Here's an adventure I had in the woods."

BOOK EXPLORING

Have students write about the point of view used in their books. They should tell who the narrator is, and they should include excerpts with the pronouns that illustrate the viewpoint.

THE LEAD

This way to thrills and spills.

The *lead* (pronounced "leed") is a story's beginning. It aims to catch the reader's attention. Leads can be categorized by their content:

Action leads show something happening. For example: Little Red Riding Hood wrapped a cake for her grandmother.

Character leads describe appearance or personality: Little Red Riding Hood was a happy girl, who wore a red hood coat.

Dialogue leads include talk: "Bye, Mom," said Red Riding Hood as she left the cottage.

Setting leads tell where—and sometimes when—the action takes place: Little Red Riding Hood's cottage smelled of fresh-baked goodies.

Summary leads answer five questions: who? did what? where? when? why? One summer day, Little Red Riding Hood hurriedly packed some goodies which she was going to take to her sick grandma, in order to cheer her up.

The storybook models for this lesson are:

Corduroy
The Day Jimmy's Boa Ate the Wash
Goodnight Moon
Why Mosquitoes Buzz in People's Ears
William's Doll

❖ ACTIVITIES ❖

MODEL READING

List the types of leads on the board and explain them. After reading the opening of each model, ask students to identify the lead.

Action lead from *Why Mosquitoes Buzz in People's Ears*:
One morning a mosquito saw an iguana drinking at a water hole.

Character lead from *William's Doll*:
William wanted a doll.

Dialogue lead from *The Day Jimmy's Boa Ate the Wash*:
"How did your school trip go today?"

Setting lead from *Goodnight Moon*:
In the great green room
There was a telephone . . .

Summary lead from *Corduroy*:
Corduroy is a bear who once lived in the toy department of a big store.
Day after day he waited with all the other animals and dolls for somebody to come along and take him home.

Because many leads are "mixed" (for example, character plus action) there may be valid disagreements about how to classify a given opening.

LANGUAGE SCOUTING

Bring in a variety of storybooks and have students look for different types of leads. Later, they can expand their search by collecting leads found in chapter books, novels, or magazine stories. Make a bulletin board featuring the different types of leads. Note: Every chapter in a novel begins with its own lead.

STORY WRITING

Challenge students, working alone or in small groups, to think up several new leads for fairy tales, fables, or storybooks.

When students work on their own stories, encourage them to write several possible leads and then choose the one they like best. This is a strategy many successful writers use.

BOOK EXPLORING

Have each student identify the leads from the chapters of a novel. Does the writer begin every chapter in the same way, or are a variety of leads used?

The entire class might do a group research project graphing leads from books they read independently. What type of lead is most common? What type is used least often?

Descriptive writing (called the story's "narration") is a matter of creating word pictures of people, places, things, and actions. There are three steps to the process:

Seeing or imagining the subject: The writer observes or mentally pictures the subject before describing it.

Choosing a focus: The writer decides what's most important about the subject, for example, that the subject is "a noisy room" or "a friendly bear." A useful strategy is to state what the focus is in two or three words.

Choosing supporting details: From the dozens or hundreds of facts about the subject, the writer chooses just a few to bring the picture into focus. For example, the key details about the Big Bad Wolf are his "big eyes," his "big ears," and especially his "big teeth."

Because the best storybooks are filled with first-rate images, these books are useful for training the writer's eye.

The storybook model for this lesson is:

Where the Wild Things Are

❖ ACTIVITIES ❖

MODEL READING

After reading *Where the Wild Things Are*, have students identify important descriptive details found in both the text and the art. For example:

Subject	Details
forest in Max's room	vines, trees, bushes, flowers
sea voyage	waves, wind, sea monster
Wild Things	roars, gnashing teeth, rolling eyes, terrible claws

LANGUAGE SCOUTING

Have students, working alone or in small groups, go through a storybook, looking for verbal or visual details that show the essential features of characters, settings, things, and actions. They should take notes, for example:

> The main action is set in a beautiful house. Examples of the house's beauty are its beautiful orchard and its stained glass windows.

Each group can present its findings to the whole class.

STORY WRITING

Each student translates some or all of the pictures in a storybook into descriptive passages. The goal is to create word pictures that enable readers to "see" what's going on without looking at the illustrations.

Later, suggest that students use newspaper and magazine pictures—of people, places, things, and actions—as starting points for word pictures in their stories. Note: Many professional writers use this technique. Rather than invent images from scratch, they borrow from ready-made pictures.

Students could also make their own sketches of settings, characters, and actions in their stories. Even stick-figure sketches can help focus word pictures.

BOOK EXPLORING

Have students find and discuss a few important word pictures found in their independent-reading books. They might choose passages that describe:

- the hero or other central characters
- the main setting
- the key action or event

Students might look for key words and phrases at the heart of each image. Often, these will be nouns and verbs.

Another option is for students to draw pictures based on word pictures found in their books. This kind of translation encourages careful reading of the text. The finished illustrations might be shared on a bulletin board.

DIALOGUE

Like people in the real world, storybook characters talk. Their talk is called dialogue. Some of the most memorable writing in literature is dialogue:

- "The sky is falling! The sky is falling."
- "This porridge is too hot. And this porridge is too cold. But . . ."
- "Oh, Grandma, what big teeth you have!"

Points to remember when writing dialogue are:

- Use **quotation marks.** Quotation marks (" ") add clarity by separating dialogue from the rest of the text.
- Use **dialogue tags.** Phrases such as *he asked quietly* or *she stated boldly* identify who's talking. They can also be used to indicate a character's tone of voice.
- **Put each new speech in its own paragraph.**
- **Avoid small talk.** Four kinds of usually interesting dialogue are: questions, threats, commands, and eye-witness observations.

The storybook models for this lesson are:

Caps for Sale
The Day Jimmy's Boa Ate the Wash
Is Your Mama a Llama?

❖ ACTIVITIES ❖

MODEL READING

Define "dialogue" as story talk. Then read and compare the use of dialogue in *Caps for Sale*, *Is Your Mama a Llama?*, and *The Day Jimmy's Boa Ate the Wash*. The first book uses dialogue conventionally, mixing it with description. The second book features questioning dialogue. The third is unusual because all the text is dialogue.

LANGUAGE SCOUTING

List several types of dialogue on the board and explain each one. Then bring in a variety of storybooks and have students, working independently or in small groups, look for examples of each kind. They can then share their discoveries with the whole class. Some categories of interest are:

> questions: "Mirror, mirror, on the wall, who's the fairest of them all?"
> threats: "I'll huff and I'll puff and I'll blow your house down."
> commands: "Rapunzel, Rapunzel, let down your long hair."
> observations: "Fe, fi, fo, fum, I smell the blood of an Englishman."

Another project is for students to collect dialogue tags, the short phrases that give the following information:

> who's talking: "It's raining," <u>Sandy</u> said.
> volume: "It's raining," someone <u>whispered</u>.
> tone of voice: "It's raining," he said <u>bitterly</u>.
> who is addressed: "It's raining," Nelson said <u>to Martha</u>.

Make a bulletin board showing examples of different uses of dialogue tags.

STORY WRITING

Have students experiment with synonyms for *said* (asked, complained, hissed, explained, shouted, threatened, whispered, etc.) by writing tags for dialogue in comic-strip balloons, or tags for dialogue in a story you read aloud. Note: Overly creative tagging can distract readers. Most experienced writers use *said* in most cases. They use other tag words sparingly, almost as a spice.

Older students might enjoy the challenge of writing an entire story in dialogue.

BOOK EXPLORING

Have students study dialogue in books they read independently. They then can graph the frequency of tag words.

❖ MORE MODELS ❖

STORYBOOKS

POINT OF VIEW—FIRST PERSON
- *And to Think That I Saw It on Mulberry Street*
- *The Bicycle Man*
- *The Cat in the Hat*
- *The Cat in the Hat Comes Back*
- *The Tenth Good Thing About Barney*

FORM—RHYME
- *Casey at the Bat*
- *The Cat in the Hat*
- *The Cat in the Hat Comes Back*
- *Horton Hatches the Egg*
- *Is Your Mama a Llama?*
- *Madeline*
- *Never Talk to Strangers*
- *There'll Be a Hot Time in the Old Town Tonight*

TONE—COMICAL
- *Alexander and the Terrible, Horrible, No Good, Very Bad Day*
- *And to Think That I Saw It on Mulberry Street*
- *The Cat in the Hat*
- *The Day Jimmy's Boa Ate the Wash*
- *The 500 Hats of Bartholomew Cubbins*
- *Horton Hatches the Egg*
- *If You Give a Mouse a Cookie*
- *Ira Sleeps Over*
- *Madeline*
- *The True Story of the 3 Little Pigs! by A. Wolf*
- *Where the Wild Things Are*

FICTION

POINT OF VIEW—FIRST PERSON
- *Ghosts I Have Been*
- *Sarah, Plain and Tall*
- *Tales of a Fourth Grade Nothing*

TONE—COMICAL
- *Alice's Adventures in Wonderland*
- *Charlie and the Chocolate Factory*
- *The Phantom Tollbooth*
- *Tales of a Fourth Grade Nothing*

❖ BIBLIOGRAPHY ❖

STORYBOOKS

Alexander and the Terrible, Horrible, No Good, Very Bad Day by Judith Viorst, il. by Ray Cruz (Atheneum, 1972). So many things go wrong, the hero considers moving to Australia, but his mother says that everyone has bad days, even in Australia.

The Amazing Bone by William Steig (Farrar, Straus, 1976). Going home from school, a pig named Pearl finds a talking bone, lost by a witch. The bone saves Pearl from robbers, but then a fox captures Pearl and plans to make her his dinner. At the last moment, the bone recalls magical phrases that shrink the fox to mouse size. Pearl and the bone become lasting friends.

And to Think That I Saw It on Mulberry Street by Dr. Seuss (Random House, 1964). A young boy sees an ordinary horse and wagon which, in his imagination, become a grand circus parade. Told in rhyme.

The Bicycle Man by Allen Say (Houghton Mifflin, 1982). An American soldier delights Japanese children with amazing bicycle tricks.

Caps for Sale by Esphyr Slobodkina (Scott, 1940). Monkeys steal all but one of a peddler's caps. Unable to coax the monkeys out of a tree, the peddler throws his cap down. When the monkeys imitate the man, he gets his caps.

Casey at the Bat by Ernest Thayer, il. by Patricia Polacco (orig. 1888, Putnam's, 1988). An arrogant baseball hero strikes out. Told in rhyme.

The Cat in the Hat by Dr. Seuss (Random House, 1957). On a rainy day, two kids are visited by a playful cat who turns the house upside down, but then picks everything up just before Mother returns. Told in rhyme.

The Cat in the Hat Comes Back by Dr. Seuss (Random House, 1958). More mischief from the Cat. Told in rhyme.

Corduroy by Don Freeman (Viking, 1968). A toy bear is given a home by a loving little girl.

Curious George by H.A. Rey (Houghton Mifflin, 1941). George, a monkey, arrives in the U.S. His curiosity lands him in prison. Following an escape and a balloon flight, George willingly moves to the zoo.

The Day Jimmy's Boa Ate the Wash by Trinka Nobel, il. by Steven Kellogg (Dial, 1980). A class trip to the farm turns into chaos thanks to a pet boa. The humor derives from the backward telling of the plot.

The 500 Hats of Bartholomew Cubbins by Dr. Seuss (Random House, 1938). When hats eerily appear on his head, young Bartholomew is in danger of losing his head.

George and Martha by James Marshall (Houghton Mifflin, 1972). Two hippos explore lying, peeking, and other barriers to friendship.

Goodnight Moon by Margaret Wise Brown, il. by Clement Hurd (Harper & Row, 1947). A bunny gets ready for sleep. Told in rhyme.

Horton Hatches the Egg by Dr. Seuss (Random House, 1940). Mayzie, a lazy bird, gets Horton, an elephant, to sit on her egg. Horton perseveres through many hardships. Months later, Mayzie claims the egg. But the elephant-like hatchling bonds with Horton.

If You Give a Mouse a Cookie by Laura Joffee Numeroff, il. by Felicia Bond (HarperCollins, 1985). The narrator shows how one act of kindness can lead to a relationship.

Ira Sleeps Over by Bernard Waber (Houghton Mifflin, 1972). Ira debates whether or not to bring his teddy on his first sleep-over. His sister convinces him that he'll look foolish. That night, Ira learns that his host holds a bear for comfort, and Ira gets his bear.

Is Your Mama a Llama? by Deborah Guarino, il. by Steven Kellogg (Scholastic, 1989). A young llama asks animal friends, "Is your mama a llama?" The answer is always "No," until the llama meets one of its own kind.

The Island of the Skog by Steven Kellogg (Dial, 1973). A group of mice seek a cat-free life. After a rough voyage, they are scared by a Skog, who turns out to be a gentle creature.

The Little Engine That Could retold by Watty Piper, il. by George and Doris Hauman (Platt & Munk, 1930). Confidence enables an engine to handle a tough challenge.

The Little House by Virginia Lee Burton (Houghton Mifflin, 1942). A country cottage wants to live in the city. After decades, the city surrounds and damages the house. New owners then return the house to the country.

Madeline by Ludwig Bemelmans (Simon & Schuster, 1939). A girl in a Paris orphanage has an adventure in a hospital. Told in rhyme.

Make Way for Ducklings by Robert McCloskey (Viking, 1941). Mrs. Mallard leads her ducklings through town, where they have adventures crossing busy streets on their way to a beautiful park.

Mike Mulligan and His Steam Shovel by Virginia Lee Burton (Houghton Mifflin, 1939). To prove his steam shovel "Mary Anne" can compete against new machines, Mike digs the cellar for Popperville's new town hall in one day. When Mike forgets to leave a way out of the cellar, a boy offers a solution: Mary Anne becomes the building's furnace.

Mr. and Mrs. Pig's Evening Out by Mary Rayner (Atheneum, 1976). The Pig parents carelessly hire Mrs. Wolf to baby-sit. For a snack, Mrs. Wolf snatches one piglet from his bed. The other nine piglets rescue their brother. Father Pig dumps Mrs. Wolf into the river: She is not heard of again "for a very long time."

Never Talk to Strangers by Irma Joyce, il. by George Buckett (Golden Press, 1967). Two kids handle dangers. Told in rhyme.

Ox-Cart Man by Donald Hall, il. by Barbara Cooney (Puffin, 1979). A 19th-century family lives through the seasons.

The Red Balloon by A. Lamorisse (Doubleday, 1956). A boy befriends a balloon, which is attacked by bad boys. Tragedy turns to joy.

The Snowy Day by Ezra Jack Keats (Viking, 1962). A little boy has fun in the snow.

Stevie by John Steptoe (Harper & Row, 1969). Robert is forced to care for Stevie, a family friend's child. Robert views Stevie as a pest until Stevie moves away.

Strega Nona retold by Tomie de Paola (Prentice-Hall, 1975). When Big Anthony steals Strega Nona's magic secret, chaos results.

The Tale of Peter Rabbit by Beatrix Potter (Warne, 1902). A naughty rabbit raids Mr. McGregor's garden and nearly meets his end.

The Tenth Good Thing About Barney by Judith Viorst, il. by Erik Blegvad (Atheneum, 1971). A boy deals with his cat's death by celebrating the cat's good qualities.

There'll Be a Hot Time in the Old Town Tonight retold by Robert Quackenbush (Lippincott, 1974). A cow causes a famous fire. Told in rhyme.

There's a Nightmare in My Closet by Mercer Mayer (Dial, 1968). A child confronts his nightmare and triumphs over fear.

The True Story of the 3 Little Pigs! by A. Wolf by Jon Scieszka, il. by Lane Smith (Viking, 1989). The Big Bad Wolf tells his side of the story. No surprise, he comes out as the innocent victim of the impolite pigs.

Where the Wild Things Are by Maurice Sendak (Harper & Row, 1963). After making mischief and being sent to bed without supper, Max enters a dream world where he visits the "Wild Things." In the end, Max misses his home.

Why Mosquitoes Buzz in People's Ears by Verna Aardema, il. by Leo and Diane Dillon (Dial, 1975). The animals learn how one little lie can lead to big trouble.

William's Doll by Charlotte Zolotow, il. by William Du Bois (Harper, 1972). Despite the teasing of his friends, a young boy asks for a doll to play with, so that he can learn to nurture his own child some day.

FICTION

The Adventures of Pinocchio by Carlo Collodi (Four Winds, 1981). A wooden puppet struggles to become a real boy.

Alice's Adventures in Wonderland by Lewis Carroll (1865). Fantastic characters, met during a dream journey, teach a girl about reality.

The Black Stallion by Walter Farley (Random House, 1941). A great thoroughbred wins races while its young owner solves mysteries.

The Borrowers by Mary Norton (Harcourt, 1953). A family of tiny people, who live under the floor, use normal-size things to get along.

Bridge to Terabithia by Katherine Paterson (Crowell, 1977). A boy and girl form a friendship and share a secret hiding place. The girl's death forces the boy to confront reality.

Charlie and the Chocolate Factory by Roald Dahl (Knopf, 1964). A good boy, joined by a troupe of outrageously bad children, explores Willie Wonka's fabulous Chocolate Factory.

Charlotte's Web by E.B. White (Harper, 1952). A lovable pig, Wilbur, is saved from death by a heroic spider.

The Children's Homer by Padraic Colum (Macmillan, 1918). This prose version of Homer's *The Iliad* and *The Odyssey* allows kids to enjoy two of literature's greatest adventures.

The Dark Is Rising by Susan Cooper (McElderry, 1973). A fantasy journey that pits good against evil.

Ghosts I Have Been by Richard Peck (Viking, 1977). The heroine travels back in time to solve a mystery rooted in the sinking of the *Titanic*.

James and the Giant Peach by Roald Dahl (Knopf, 1961). A boy uses fantasy to escape from an unhappy life.

Julie of the Wolves by Jean Craighead George (Harper, 1972). A 13-year-old Eskimo girl, lost on the tundra, is saved by wolves.

The Lion, the Witch, and the Wardrobe by C.S. Lewis (Macmillan, 1950). The forces of good and evil do battle.

Mrs. Frisbee and the Rats of NIMH by Robert O'Brien (Atheneum, 1971). Super-intelligent rats, created by scientists at the National Institute of Mental Health, build a society.

Paddle-to-the-Sea by Holling C. Holling (Houghton Mifflin, 1941). A toy canoe, carrying a toy Indian, navigates the waterways on a journey to the Atlantic.

The Phantom Tollbooth by Norton Juster (Random House, 1961). A young boy enters a fantasy world where he learns about science, logic, and the threat of ignorance.

Roll of Thunder, Hear My Cry by Mildred Taylor (Dial, 1976). A Depression-era poor black family in Mississippi struggles to maintain their dignity.

Sarah, Plain and Tall by Patricia MacLachlan (Harper, 1985). A girl's account of the romance between her widowed father and a woman who joins the family on their ranch.

Tales of a Fourth Grade Nothing by Judy Blume (Dutton, 1972). A nine-year-old boy describes his middle-class urban life.

Tuck Everlasting by Natalie Babbitt (Farrar, Straus, 1975). A ten-year-old girl builds an impossible friendship with a playmate who has acquired the secret of eternal life.

The Wonderful Wizard of Oz by Frank Baum (Morrow, 1900). After visiting a fabled land, a young Kansas girl discovers that "there's no place like home."

❖ INDEX ❖